Gaslit By A Madman: Illuminated Poems

I think, therefore I am mad. —Max Lewy

Independently Published

Copyright © Max J. Lewy
November 2019

ABOUT THE BOOK

GASLITBYAMADMAN, "The Certifiably TRUE Ravings Of A Sectioned Philosopher", is a droller take on the subjects of mental health, political issues and Nietzschean, Christian, Jungian, existentialist and post-modern philosophy. Don't be afraid to question your world view, don't be afraid to think you might be a bit 'mad'. Who isn't?

It is based on the author, Max J. Lewy's, own experience as an oh-so-patient patient in the N.H.S. Mental Health System. Veritably knocked off his horse by two out-of-control, gaslighting shrinks at the tender age of 23, his writings trace his recovery from this life-changing, iatrogenic incident over the next 12 or so years, exploring the 'mad' identity that was placed upon him and the truly insane, or certainly very flawed and eye-brow raising System which so unfortunately often does such things to quite healthy and relatively rational people. This companion volume, released on his 36th (that's 6 x 6) birthday as a little gift (for "The Beast", presumably... but who knows, maybe Lucifer, maybe Jesus, maybe the old bearded madman at the end of the street with an "The Apocalypse Is Nigh" cardboard sign hung to the back of his bike.), contains 36 beautifully illuminated poems, in the manner of William Blake, only with modern-day collaged images from around the world wide web.

***

Madness has always fascinated and terrified the mind of man, in equal measure. In today's medicalized, 'normalized' world, it has come to be seen simply as a 'disease', an ugly blight on the smooth, cog-like operation of the social organism. Our very language has become impoverished by the steady stream of scientistic neologisms which have rushed to take its stead, leaving us with only the cold apparatus of an all-too suspect, bullying and anti-septic 'reason'. Once the most intimate bedfellow not only of depthless despair, but also of high ecstasy and genius, we seem to have all but forgotten the myriad enchantments with which this fateful 'daimon' – to quote Socrates - once tempted us. This book is both a chronicling of the author's own personal voyage through such altered states of conscious, through to the far greater, far more intimidating battle with the very system that was allegedly put in place to try to 'heal' him. Here is his invitation to all sufferers and practitioners alike to glimpse beyond the borders of the straight-jacketed, dysfunctional status quo, and just maybe rekindle that sense of mystery and magic, the sense of possibility, once associated with this most uncanny and uncompromising of guests. At times an exuberant Jubilee to pure lunacy, at others a scathing, disabused presentation of the current 'Mental Health' establishment, and at still others as melancholy, cathartic a song as the trail of Dionysus's adoring attendants: 'Madness: a form of love' is a gambit not to anesthetize and sedate our 'dangerous gifts', but to joyfully embrace them - and with them our own secret innermost selves - to live authentically in light of the absurd, inconvenient, M.A.D. (short for 'Miracles A Dozen') truths of our existence.

(Caution: This book contains POETRY, side-effects include ecstatic, trance-like states, life-changing epiphanies, rebellious outrage, vomiting up society's propaganda, foaming at the mouth, increased working vocabulary, uncontrollable weeping or laughter, mild shortness of breath and slight dizziness!)

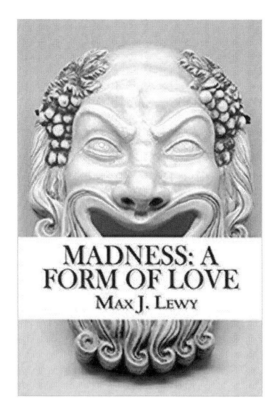

Available online at:

ALL AMAZON WORLDWIDE SITES

www.amazon.co.uk
www.amazon.com
www.amazon.ca
www.amazon.com.au
www.amazon.co.jp

…………..and more

ACKNOWLEDGEMENTS

Thank you to those who have supported me without having received anything in return, especially the great previous writers & poets - precious, rare voices of sanity amid History's cruel, seemingly idiot cacophony - who inspired me and led me to express myself at all.

Also many thanks to my friend from India for helping me put this together in a publishable format, & especially my first book, from which these poems are drawn, without which publication & the resulting unexpected victory in RealisticPoetry's 2018 Perspectives Of Love contest, I'd probably still be being crucified by the 'medical profession' and utterly lost, dysfunctional & miserable.

Thank you to the one or two doctors and nurses who have done their little bit to extricate me from that situation which the original doctors threw me into for years and years.

CONTENTS / INDEX

Madness: a form of love

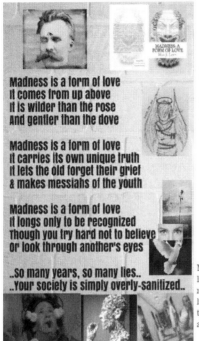

Madness is a form of love
It comes from up above
It is wilder than the rose
And gentler than the dove

Madness is a form of love
It carries its own unique truth
It lets the old forget their grief
And makes messiahs of the youth

Madness is a form of love
It longs only to be recognised
Though you try hard not to believe
Or look through another's eyes

...So many years, so many lies...
...Your society is simply overly-sanitized...

He Strove

He strove against world, and all the lethargy it contains,
THe doleful march of men unable to see beyond their little lanes,
He strove against the moon, Relentless ruler of the tide,
He swore that when his fate'd come, he'd be ready just in time;
He strove against the land, the air, the sun, the sea,
The little folk who laugh, and throw stones at you and me
He strove against the grain, he strove against the sand,
He hoped to build a magic fortress and do it all by his mind;
He strove against the pull,   he strove against the tow, -- Of a
thousand years --

He said that its the stubbornest men, who have the best careers.
He strove so long, so hard, so proud, against shallow conformity,
The sorry thing was, -- so exhausted with striving was he --
                he never did leave his dormitory!

MADNESS: A
FORM OF LOVE
MAX J. LEWY

Poetry Not Pills

**About the
author:**

Max J. Lewy is the author of 'Madness: a form
love'. A mad-eyed lunatic residing in the
mytho-poetic South Wales valleys, letting
loose exquisitely choreographed 'howls' against
the Mental Hellth System that has so reduced
and depraved him. Follow on Twitter :
@ PillPuppetPoet

He strove against the world, and all the lethargy it contains,
The doleful march of men unable to see beyond their little lanes.
He strove against the moon, Relentless ruler of the tide,
He swore that when his fate'd come, he'd be ready just in time;
He strove against the land, the air, the sun, the sea,
The little folk who laugh, and throw stones at you and me;
He strove against the grain, he strove against the sand,
He hoped to build a magic fortress and do it all by his mind;
He strove against the pull, he strove against the tow, - Of a thousand years
-
He said that its the stubbornest men, who have the best careers.
He strove so long, so hard, so proud, against shallow conformity,
The sorry thing was, - so exhausted with striving was he - he never did
leave his dormitory!

In The Garden

They don't twitch a muscle until you're dead,
Until all your gold has turned to lead -
Safely buried, in the garden of Mystery.

In the Womb of Nothingness;
The Tomb of all our Hopes,
Where lost loves forever Bloom:
Obsolete but unsullied,
Unmarked, perfectly intact.

Then they spoil your rest with their weeping,
Their reflexes become activated.

Orchid

 Orchid

A chill triumvirate of diadems,
Amid pirouettes of billowing mist,
Lit only, by black-laced thread.
Rememberance, the nightly detour
Of obsidian osmosis.

Watching your sweet heart palpate
Away, in dank, black uncelebrated shades.
Regret stands on every altar. We shiver together prone in
But -- ah ! --   the wind...
Hijack the moon! -
You are my first and last   As a monsoon lifts her Poetry Not Pills
                              ankles,
        soliloquy.   And begins to waltz across
                                the skies. About the
Without lustre, lacking liberty,
Lanturne of laconic intermissions.   author:
Listen! There flits a dragonfly,
        On its way to the stars.   Tears of crystal, only friend.

Max J. Lewy is the author of "Madness: a form
Lo! A maniacal masquerade.   love". A mad-eyed lunatic residing in the
                                          mytho-poetic South Wales valleys, letting
                                          loose exquisitely choreographed 'howls' against
                                          the Mental Hellth System that has so reduced
                                          and depraved him. Follow on Twitter :
The play of the sleepwalkers,   @ PillPuppetPoet
Ghosts, with coffee-ed out souls..

MADNESS: A
FORM OF LOVE
MAX J. LEWY

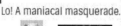

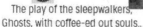

A chill triumvirate of diadems,
Amid pirouettes of billowing mist,
Lit by black-laced thread.
Remembrance, the nightly detour
Of obsidian osmosis.

Watching your sweet heart palpate
Away, in dank, black uncelebrated shades.
Regret stands on every altar.
But -ah !-
Hijack the moon! -
You are my first and last

soliloquy.

Without lustre, lacking liberty,
Lanturne of laconic intermissions.
Listen! There flits a dragonfly,
On its way to the stars.

Lo ! A maniacal masquerade.

The play of the sleepwalkers;
Ghosts, with coffee-ed out souls...

We shiver together prone in the wind...
As a monsoon lifts her ankles,
And begins to waltz across the skies.

Tears of crystal, only friend.

Lunar Portal

Upon a distant planet, stratosphere long since vanished,
Blue florescent light floats, gleaming amid the ruins,
Scarlet foliage, of some unknown, alien variegation,
Growing up along their ancient walls,
Within which our strange race one dwelt.
A passage way of peerless pitch,
Yawns open as night beneath a marble mantle.
Take a leap, into the wild weird:
Madness beckons, a cosmos of untold beauty,
Secret portal to new, fathomless destiny,
Hewn of Sphinx-like mystery,
Awaiting thine footsteps since time immemorial.
Calling to the intrepid explorer,
Archaeologist of a long forgotten, past life
Stirred only by deja vu.

Tiny Little Pill

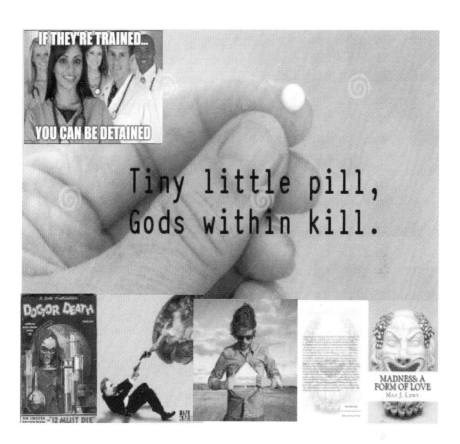

Tiny little pill
Gods within kill

Lobotomised The Beast

Lobotomized The Beast

They come from within,
Come over us like lightening,
When once we weere men --
Not as concrete beings or voices talking in our ear, as they stupidly,
self-servingly assume;
On our subtler, yett loftier tongues
(We who imbue humanity with its proper dignity, which stretches
To the divine -- which, in a sense, is itself man-made or man-killed.)
Such words bespeak impersonal, inner energies, activities
And potentialities --
Just as 'gravity' names an outer energy.
They are psychologiccal archetypes,
Not angels or demons in outward form, descending from the skies
which only we can see!
Why use such loaded terms, you say, such as 'angels on wing'?
Because they have poetic force.
And the spirit longs to sing!
Now we only have another type of electrical intercession to look
forward to.
What use is joyful rhyme against such brute contingencies?
In their mean eyes, a dance is a mere fit.
Meditation? An aberration...
To those seeking 'help'
"Get out before you get caught, and lend a hand to those who
weren't so lucky."
For who will help them who need help (to flee) from their 'helpers'?
Who can even see which way the earth truly revolves here, let alone
alter its agonizing axis?

Since psychiatry came to me,
I drool like a dog in my dreams.
Since psychiatry came to me,
I drool like a dog,
Even in my dreams.
Since psychiatry caged little old me,
Everything is even worse than it seems,
Since psychiatry was let loose on me,
Everything is just as bad as it seems,
Seems in my dreams.
They talk over me, even in my dreams,
'til I'm nearly bursting at the seams.
There is no use for screams...
Once there was a Christ-force that dwelt within,
Now grown pale and ghostly thin,
The kernel has been cored-out!
But it doesn't matter how we shout..
666/888
The devil, the seducer of the world/
THe Word, the prince of his own soul!
They're all the same -- They're all gods.

Continued...

Lobotomized The Beast Part II
by Max J. Lewy

I am just a toy, the least of creatures -- begging, barking for dignity
Dignity in defeat
Like their forebearers, the priests and Inquisitors of old:
The shrinks have carved up my savior for tea,
To be sold,
For the sake of their foolish feast --
A meal of vanity and greed
They have even lobotmized The Beast.
Theirs is a religion stunted of both notion and emotion,
Its charisma is like a poorly made wax-work dummy,
Guache and deathly cold, yet smooth in all its juvenile simplicity,
It would make you too into a mannquin,
An exemplary ticklist of outer inconsequentialities to set beside
every barren, burning soul.
For they care about only what thwy see, they see nothing important,
And all they do is smoke and mirrors. They never awoke.
Because,
Whenever there is a soul burning, MOST PEOPLE ONLY SEE THE SMOKE.

Since psychiatry came to me,
I drool like a dog in my dreams.
Since psychiatry came to me,
I drool like a dog,
Even in my dreams.

Since psychiatry caged little old me,
Everything is even worse than it seems.
Since psychiatry was let loose on me,
Everything is just as bad as it seems,
Seems in my dreams.

They talk over me, even in my dreams,
'til I'm nearly bursting at the seems.
There is no use for screams...

Once there was a Christ-force that dwelt within,
Now grown pale and ghostly thin.
The kernel has been cored-out!
But it doesn't matter how we shout...

666/ 888.
The devil, the seducer of the world/
The Word, the prince of his own soul!
They're all the same - They're all gods.

They come from within,
Come over us like lightening,
When once we were men -
Not as concrete beings or voices talking in our ear, as they stupidly, self-
servingly assume;
On our subtler, yet loftier tongues
(We who imbue humanity with its proper dignity, which stretches to the
divine - which, in a sense, is itself man-made or man-killed..)
Such words bespeak impersonal, inner energies, activities
And potentialities -
Just as 'gravity' names an outer energy.
They are psychological principles or archetypes,

Not angels or demons in outward form, descending from the skies which
only we can see!
Why use such loaded terms, you say, such as 'angels on wing'?
Because they have poetic force...
And the spirit longs to sing !

Now we only have another type of electrical intercession to look forward
to.
What use is joyful rhyme against such contingencies?
In their mean eyes, a dance is a mere fit.
Meditation? An aberration..

To those seeking 'help' -
"Get out before you get caught, and lend a hand to those who weren't so
lucky."
For who will help them who need help (to flee) from their 'helpers' ?
Who can even see which way the earth truly revolves here, let alone alter
its agonizing axis?

I am just a toy, the least of creatures - begging, barking for dignity,
Dignity in defeat.
Like their forebearers, the priests and Inquisitors of old:
The shrinks have carved up my saviour for tea,
To be sold.
For the sake of their foolish feast -
A meal of vanity and greed -
They have even lobotomised The Beast.
Theirs is a religion stunted of both notion and emotion,
Its charisma is like a poorly made wax-work dummy,
Gauche and deathly cold, yet smooth in all its juvenile simplicity.
It would make you too into a mannequin,
An exemplary ticklist of outer inconsequentialities to set beside every
barren, burning soul.
For they care about only what they see, they see nothing important,
And all they do is smoke and mirrors. They never awoke.
Because,
Wherever there is a soul burning, *most people only see the smoke!*

Love Is Not Blind

Love Is Not Blind

Love is not undiscriminating.
Love is not blind.
Love has subtle understanding.
Love has the most attentive eyes.

Love is judicious with its giving.
It nurtures the good and beautiful ones.
And uproots the weeds.

Love has a preference for the truly living.
It hardens its heart to the hopeless.
And pushes the teetering off cliffs.

by Max J. Lewy

"Madness: a form of love"

O Love, do not be wasteful;
O Love, so precious and rare;
Ever eschewing sanctimony and shallow praise.
With your gaze full ablaze on the morrow.

Love is not undiscriminating,
Love is not blind.
Love has subtle understanding,
Love has the most attentive eyes.

Love is judicious with its giving,
It nurtures the beautiful ones,
And uproots the weeds.
Love has a preference for the truly living,
It hardens its heart to the hopeless,
And pushes the teetering off cliffs.

O, Love, do not be wasteful;
O, Love, so precious and rare;
Ever eschewing sanctimony and shallow praise,
With your gaze full ablaze on the morrow.

Thoughts Of The Unborn

Thoughts Of The Unborn

So, finally, I AM.
I am ! The universe is alive.
It's my mum.
The world is a throbbing hive,
And I am the Queen bee.
It is made to comfort me.

A multiform, rippling tapestry of veins and nerves,
Support and nourish each for my incipient verves.
It has been like this since the first moment I can remember.
I suck from a cord in my tummy,
And am granted sustenance so warm and yummy!

There is little need to cheat or dissemble.
No need to pretend I'm not hurt, by the lies that you assert,
And the chemicals that you insert.

I know you love me.

Still, with each new passing day,
My hunger grows without delay.
I have already learned to wage war
For the sake of having more, more, more.

TBC...

Poetry Not Pills

MADNESS: A FORM OF LOVE
Max J. Lewy

About the author:

Max J. Lewy is the author of 'Madness: a form love'. A mad-eyed lunatic residing in the mytho-poetic South Wales valleys, letting loose exquisitely choreographed 'howls' against the Mental Hellth System that has so reduced and depraved him. Follow on Twitter : @ PillPuppetPoet

Thougths Of The Unborn Pt. 2

I summon my strength and send out signals of distress,
Letting life know in must make expiations
For getting me in this sticky mess.

I sit snugly in this little patch,
And snatch and snatch and snatch.

Still it usually yields to the pinings my will wields.

Somehow... I have this dream of wide-open fields,
Starry skies, hopes the penetrate beyond all whys.

Yet even now, I can already smell my necessary demise.

Just as I now joyously grow, soon, I can sense it,
I will be over-run by woe. My existence is a piece of
Brute injustice, of which I am both victim and
perpetrator, righted only by the decompolsiton of
Passing years.

So let it not shock you, if I mark my new arrival with
Much blood, and many tears!

Poetry Not Pills

MADNESS: A FORM OF LOVE
Max J. Lewy

About the author:

Max J. Lewy is the author of 'Madness: a form love'. A mad-eyed lunatic residing in the mytho-poetic South Wales valleys, letting loose exquisitely choreographed 'howls' against the Mental Hellth System that has so reduced and depraved him. Follow on Twitter : @ PillPuppetPoet

So, finally, I am.
I am! The universe is alive.
It's my mum.
The world is a throbbing hive,
And I am the Queen bee.
It is made to comfort me.

A multiform, rippling tapestry of veins and nerves,
Support and nourish each of my incipient verves.
It has been like this since the first moment I can remember,
I suck from a cord in my tummy,
And am granted sustenance so warm and yummy!

There is little need to cheat or dissemble.
No need to pretend I'm not hurt, by the lies that you assert,
And the chemicals that you insert.

I know you love me.

Still, with each new passing day,
My hunger grows without delay.
I have already learned to wage war
For the sake of having more, more, more.

I summon my strength and send out signals of distress
Letting life know
It must make expiations for getting me in this sticky mess.

I sit snugly in this little patch,
And snatch and snatch and snatch.

Still, it usually yields to the pinings my will wields.

Somehow... I have this dream of wide-open fields,
Starry skies, hopes that penetrate beyond all whys.

But even now, I can already smell my necessary demise.

Just as I now joyously grow, soon, I can sense it,

I will be over-run by woe. My existence is a piece of
Brute injustice, of which I am both victim and
perpetrator, righted only by the decomposition of
Passing years.

So let it not shock you, if I mark my new arrival with...

Much blood, and many tears!

Picked

My grandfather was a diamond miner, down in North Africa.
One day deep at work in those dismal caves,
His bronze brown skin baptised by the hot, heavy, teary sweat,
That bled like a refreshing summer rain from mᵢd-day's labor,
A fellow miner's pick flew free from his grip;
It became a mad dervish, spiral ing effortlessly
With fate's terrible weight and necessity
Backwards towards my poor grandfather.
It's iron claw punctured him straight through the heart.

If our lives were like perfect flowers, poking upward through the
brown soil of eternity, we too would have , by now, been picked.

MADNESS: A FORM OF LOVE
Max J. Lewy

Poetry Not Pills

About the author:

Max J. Lewy is the author of 'Madness: a form
love'. A mad-eyed lunatic residing in the
mytho-poetic South Wales valleys, letting
loose exquisitely choreographed 'howls' against
the Mental Hellth System that has so reduced
and depraved him. Follow on Twitter
@ PillPuppetPoet

My grandfather was a diamond miner, down in North Africa.
One day deep at work in those dismal caves,
His bronze brown skin baptised by the hot, heavy, teary sweat,
That bled like a refreshing, summer rain from mid-day's labour,
A fellow miner's pick flew free from his grip;
It became a mad dervish, spiralling effortlessly,
With fate's terrible weight and necessity
Backwards towards my poor grandfather.
It's iron claw punctured him straight through the heart.

If our lives were like perfect flowers, poking upward through the brown
soil of eternity, we too would have, by now, been picked.

My Prospective Ubermensch

Studying "The Gay Science" on a public park bench,
When up walked a local lad, my prospective Ubermensch!
Thinking him a poor dupe of the doctrine of 'sin',
I decided to unlock the untamed beast within...

"Hark! I teach you the Superman!" -
"Alright, where's your cape?" -
"Not that one, you ignorant ape."
CRASH-WALLOP-BANG.

Phew, that was a close escape...
At least the security camera caught that ruffian on tape!
Good thing he didn't see the book - it could have been rape!

Thus ended my philosophic hunt;
You're lucky around here, if you can catch more than a grunt...

Sacred Jungle Of Dreams

Beyond the dull horizon of wakefulness,
Lies a jungle of multifaceted wonders.
I can almost touch her medicinal mystery;
Their plant-like plenitude beckons me.
If only I could penetrate this shallow film;
The pulsing propaganda of daylight hours,
When leopards languish lazily below the leaves..
And sink deeply down, hidden,
To the wild womb of even-tide's nocturnal embrace.
The healing dusk of imagination's tribalistic dance,
The refreshing aroma of midnight's herbs and flowers.
The plunging of life's buried root
And the withering of its secret wick-
Stars dripping honey-yellow and bright..
A ritual camp-fire flaring in the moonlight.

The Scapegoat

The Scapegoat

by Max James Lewy

A primitive superstition...
A mad mob craving a target for its rage...
A hive mind trapped in fear and ugliness...

Sacred refugee cast out amidst the desert,
Inner fugitive from pitiless public glare.
The part that we throw away and desert,
The forbidden side we don't dare to share.
Lucky victim of persecution and cruel hurt,
The innocent child on the sacrifical stair.

Watchful critic who is just too alert,
Bringer of tidings we just cannot bear.

..If he could rise,...
...then so can the outcast in us....

The custom that deigns to be an ought,
That is really most of all unfair.
The way people just do as they're taught
Doing wrong without so much as a care.

...If our bad habits lose their grip on us...
... Divine once more we shall be...

So much pain by ignorance is wrought,
So unhappy and guilty we are reared,
Put your past at last behind you,

@PillPuppetPoet

martyr of Greed, martyr of Lust, martyr of ignorance,
and shed for him, O you martyr of Beauty,

Your shadow, your scapegoat, your Christ,,
Your first heartfelt tear...

And Be Reborn Anew In His Authentic Image,
A Wayfaring Cosmonaught.

A primitive tribal superstition...
A mad mob craving a target for its rage....
A hive mind trapped in fear and ugliness...

Sacred refugee cast out amidst the desert;
Inner fugitive from the pitiless public glare.
The part that we throw-away and desert;
The forbidden side we don't dare to share.
Lucky victim of persecution and cruel hurt,
The innocent child on the sacrificial stair.

Watchful critic who is just too alert,
Bringer of tidings we just cannot bear.

....If He could rise...
...Then so can the outcast in us...

The custom that deigns to be an "ought",
But that is really the most of all unfair.
The way people just do as they're taught...
Doing Wrong without so much as a care.

...If our bad habits lose their grip on us...
...Divine once more we will be...

So much pain by ignorance is wrought,
So unhappy and guilty we are reared,
Put your past at last behind you,

martyr of Greed,
martyr of Lust,
martyr of Ignorance,

And shed for him, O you martyr of Beauty -
Your shadow, your scapegoat, your Christ -
Your First Heartfelt Tear...

And Be Reborn Anew In His Authentic Image,
A Wayfaring Cosmonaut.

Piloting The Soul

Piloting The Soul

When I was just a toddler,
I started *wrestling* the controls from my father.
Now, all by myself, I'm spinning 360 degree rolls!
I'm sailing through blue skies, I'm soaring through thin air.
There's nothing to catch me if I fall,
So I must heed the radar.

I must keep monitoring the wind speed --
The barometer of social nicety --
I must avoid collision with other planes.
I must keep one eye on the passengers -- my urges --
To make sure their exquisite balance remains

The earth is my theatre, my panoramic view.
My picture book, my museum,
My nature reserve, my zoo.
The options are almost inifnite,
But I must keep dead set on my course.
The map book, I binned it,
We're guided by The Force.

Why do we keep flying? Why do we not cease?
I cannot close my eyes, I cannot knoew release.
All these tiny dots of men,
So small its beyond my ken!
To the fields of rape we call History...
It is one big unwieldy mystery.

Oh! they're all blowing hot air, I'd be better off in a balloon !
But the spirit is set on ascension; we're flying to the moon...

MADNESS: A
FORM OF LOVE
MAX J. LEWY

Poetry Not Pills

About the
author:

Max J. Lewy is the author of "Madness: a form
love". A mad-eyed lunatic residing in the
mytho-poetic South Wales valleys, letting
loose exquisitely choreographed 'howls' against
the Mental Hellth System that has so reduced
and depraved him. Follow on Twitter :
@ PillPuppetPoet

When I was just a toddler,
I started *wrestling* the controls from my father.
Now, all by myself, I'm spinning 360 degree rolls!
I'm sailing through blue skies, I'm soaring in thin air.
There's nothing to catch me if I fall,
So I must heed the radar.

I must keep monitoring the wind speed,-
The barometer of social nicety -
I must avoid collision with other planes.
I must keep one eye on the passengers - my urges -
To make sure their exquisite balance remains.

The earth is my theatre, my panoramic view.
My picture book, my museum,
My nature reserve, my zoo.
The options are almost infinite,

But I must keep dead set of my course.
The map book, I binned it,
We're guided by The Force.

Why do we keep flying? Why do we not cease?
I cannot close my eyes, I cannot know release;
All these tiny dots of men,
So small its beyond my ken!
To the fields of rape we call history...
It is one big unwieldy mystery.

Oh! They're all blowing hot air, I'd be better off in a balloon!
But, still, the spirit is set on ascension; we're flying to the moon...

The Hypocritic Oath

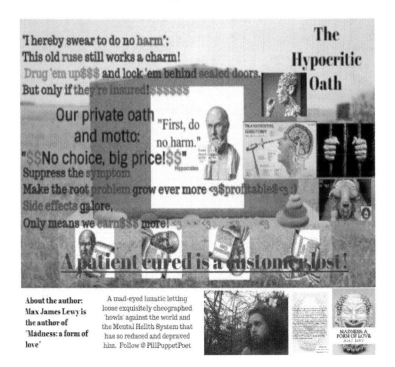

I hereby swear to do no harm.";
This old ruse still works a charm!
Drug 'em up and lock 'em behind sealed doors...
But only if they're insured!
Our private motto:
"No choice, large price!"

Suppress the symptom,
Make the root problem grow ever more profitable. :)
Side-effects galore
Only means we earn more! :)

Our private oath:
"A patient cured is a customer lost!"

Community Nurse

"Community Nurse" by M.J.L.

She is a bit eccentric, and a nice-natured lady.
Dreaming of space or time ships,
And goblins with 78 different toes.

But, when all is finally done and snipped
The party line she tows.

At predetermined intervals she visits me, like a woman's monthly woes ,
Making sure that the child inside of me, often bleeds and never grows.
"You've had your chance to burst buds in freedom", so her teacher says.
"This is for your own prudent protection, for the rest of all your days."
It seems to her a wise precaution, to nip the peaks and tuck the lows,
Because it's at an expert's inspection, someone who much better knows
Officious guardians of convention, who society's primitve fear allays.
It is for us a most difficult sentence, because ours are not their ways.

T.B.C....

She is a bit eccentric, and a nice-natured lady,
Dreaming of space or time ships,
And goblins with seventy-eight different toes.
But, when all is finally done and snipped,
The party line she tows.

At predetermined intervals she visits me, like a woman's monthly woes.
Making sure that the child inside of me, often bleeds and never grows.
"You've had your chance, to burst buds in freedom", so her teacher says.
"This is for your own prudent protection, for the rest of all your days."

23

It seems to her a wise precaution, to nip the peaks and tuck the lows.
Because its at an expert's inspection, somebody who much better knows -
Officious guardians of convention, who society's primitive fear allays.
It is for us a most difficult sentence, because ours are not their ways.

Each time she arrives, how I try and I scheme to prove myself pristinely
sane.
Yet all she probably sees is that chequered history, the hideous,
unrelenting stain.
Her lukewarm purpose melts the ice that I hold to the swollen wound in
my head.
It always seems to me that too little and yet at the same time, too much,
was said.
That harsh, baseless and unyielding verdict, that blemish against my name
-
When she leaves, I am always disappointed: same picture in the same
frame.
I do my best to affirm my resolution, how many important things I've read.
Yet afterwards I feel it was pointless, I may as well have just stayed in bed.

She says its a past of misdirection, for whom a caring judgement bell tolls.
She says its just a matter of chemistry, there's no such things as souls.
She thinks that its a better destiny, the one in which our spirit, drooling,
lulls.
She thinks winds can quickly change, there's no telling which way our
mind blows.

She is a bit eccentric, and a nice-natured lady,
Dreaming of space or time ships,
And vampires with seventy-eight different souls.
But, when all is finally done and snipped,
The party line she's sold.

Spirit's Ladder

Spirit's Ladder

Trapped beneath a ceiling full of stars,
My mind clings the contours of space,
I breathe misty air above the rat-race,
On which I'm waging a secret war.

As a neighborhood bum plays the sitar,
And an inner town road zooms with cars...
In the mystery of poverty, beneath the rags
Of luminosity, where twilight softly sags...
Above the monotony --

I scale a different bar.

Some folk think that I am sunk far below,
But to my eyes, their whys seem hollow...

Farewell, restless panic -- bile begone! --

This chilly winter night is filled with song.

MADNESS: A
FORM OF LOVE
Max J. Lewy

Poetry Not Pills

About the author:

Max J. Lewy is the author of 'Madness: a form
love'. A mad-eyed lunatic residing in the
mytho-poetic South Wales valleys, letting
loose exquisitely choreographed howls against
the Mental Health System that has so reduced
and depraved him. Follow on Twitter :
@ PillPuppetPoet

Trapped beneath a ceiling full of stars,
My mind clings the contours of space;
I breathe misty air above the rat race -
On which I am waging a secret war.

As a neighbourhood bum plays the sitar,
And an inner town road zooms with cars...
In the mystery of poverty, beneath the rags
Of luminosity, where twilight softly sags...
Above the monotony - I scale a different bar.

Some folk think that I am sunk far below,
But to my eyes, their whys seem hollow...

Farewell, restless panic – bile begone!-
This chilly winter night is filled with song.

Meeting With The Most Beautiful Angel

Knock, knock, knock!

"Hello?"

"Its Satan! I've come for your soul."
He points to the blue box in his hand. "Just slip it in here."

I decide to lend the guy an ear.

First he put on a show,
Of his opalescent visage,
His tongue eloquent beyond earthly understanding,
His she-devils seductive and maddening.

"I promise you earthly happiness-
Your ego will be walled up within the bounds of my religion forever,

Rendered docile and content, you will see nothing but skies blue as this box
With nothing to lament."

I thought to myself "This is tempting; freedom is wasted on me nowadays anyway.
But, then again, eternity is a long time to be without a soul; I cannot consent."

Then I asked him whether he was not afraid of reprisals from on high;
He merely tilted his hat and nodded goodbye.

And so he disappeared again, and I did sigh and almost did cry.

Such a remarkable fellow... rarely has come my way.

Just More Meds

MADNESS: A FORM OF LOVE
Max J. Lewy

Poetry Not Pills

The police hand-cuff me and sling me in the back of their van,
The van speeds off, I struggle to breathe and they don't give a damn.
Us damned, so-called 'demented' souls have practically no rights-
Though it might seem right, it is however self-defeating to put up a fight.
Battling for air I try to reason with the chimp behind the wheel;
Wheeling around and around like a rat in a cage of steel.
Stealing is still illegal, but kidnapping has bcome a societal norm.
Normally they all just follow orders like those Troopers-Storm.
The storm through my nerves a tempest swirls, ripping my soul to shreds.
Get lucky I'll have shreddies for breakfast, but mostly just more meds.

About the author:

Max J. Lewy is the author of "Madness: a form
love". A mad-eyed lunatic residing in the
mytho-poetic South Wales valleys, letting
loose exquisitely choreographed 'howls' against
the Mental Hellth System that has so reduced
and depraved him. Follow on Twitter :
@ PillPuppetPoet

The police hand-cuff me and sling me in the back on their van.
The van speeds off, I struggle to breathe and they don't give a damn.
Us damned, so-called demented souls have practically no rights-
Though it might seem right, it is however self-defeating to put up a fight.
Battling for air I try to reason with the chimp behind the wheel;
Wheeling around and around like a rat in a cage of steel.
Stealing is still illegal, but kidnapping has become a societal norm.
Normally they all just follow orders like those Troopers-Storm.
The storm through my nerves a tempest swirls, ripping my soul to shreds.
Get lucky I'll have shreddies for breakfast, but mostly just more meds.

Dionysus On The Dole

Dionysus On The Dole

I wear a masquerade ball mask,
And am trailed by melancholy nymphs.
Well, bi polar single mums, that is!

Riding the South wind down the town,
Leaving mayhem in my wake.
The coppers are easy to ditch,
They're hardly awake! Or on the take!

For those who have not the strength to conquer, their only
hope lies in surrender!

Wine flows freely on my lips;
We come in gulps, never sips.
Breaking the balustrade by life's river,
Making sure they all fall in.
Ecstasy, silence, pandemonium and sin.

I am the fateful diver --
Morose machismo,
Law-shattering lethargy,
Insidious inviolate inflame --

A spur of destruction and rebirth;
(And that's just this cut-throat economy!)
Collecting my welfare checks of course...

I am a god, I don't need a job.

I give the shrinks the cold shoulder;
Sure of the insanity plea, I just grow bolder!

MADNESS: A FORM OF LOVE
MAX J. LEWY

Poetry Not Pills

About the author:

Max J. Lewy is the author of 'Madness: a form
love'. A mad-eyed lunatic residing in the
mytho-poetic South Wales valleys, letting
loose exquisitely choreographed 'howls' against
the Mental Hellth System that has so reduced
and depraved him. Follow on Twitter :
@ PillPuppetPoet

I wear a masquerade ball mask,
And am trailed by melancholy nymphs.
Well, bi-polar single mums, that is!

Riding the South wind down the town,
Leaving mayhem in my wake.
The coppers are easy to ditch,
They're hardly awake! Or on the take!

For those who have not the strength to conquer, their only hope lies in
surrender!

***

Wine flows freely on my lips;
We come in gulps, never sips.
Breaking the balustrade by life's river,
Making sure they all fall in.
Ecstasy, silence, pandemonium and sin.

I am the fateful diver -
Morose machismo,
Law-shattering lethargy,
Insidious inviolate inflame -

A spur of destruction and rebirth;
(And that's just this cut-throat economy!)
Collecting my welfare checks of course...

I am a god, I don't need a job.

I bring madness, I bring joy.
I stir you into incensed rage like a toy.
Why am I not hunched? Why am I so elated?
Why do I have the nerve to lay low and yet resist unabated?

I give the shrinks the cold shoulder;
Sure of an insanity plea, I just grow bolder!

Hearing From History

Save your paltry prayers for one who cares,
I'll be the one pushing them off the stairs!
You could spend all night embellishing me with your tears.
At the beginning of the new day,
You'll still find me marring your precious careers,
With the jeers of one who cheers not for the gainful 'nears',
But the faraway suns.

The ones which flare and die,
Not in the instant of your debauched sigh,
But under the aspect of eternal jubilee
Do forever rise.

You say 'that's just' me,
In your fetid, faithless eye its all a matter of relativity,
But wait and see,
What goes around comes around:
Get off your settee and join the ranks of the free
Or you'll be hearing from History!

City Sage

City Sage

Shunned by the trance laden masses,
Spat upon by the self-appointed 'elite'.
Just around some dirty corner street
In every major city, even today,
In his sleeping bag curled up within
Some dusty back alley passage way...
A Buddha patiently dwells --
Waiting for the world's Holy Wonder to re-awaken.

By lying low on crowded streets,
I rise like warm vapours from vents in the pavement,
Above the multitudinous mind.
I have, I am -- everything and nothing:
My words shout surrender, but my voice is filled with design;
Without a penny to my name, the entire city is my boudoir.
For them it is a battleground of all against all.
But pity and gratitude are the portion on which I survive;
Handouts to my cupped palms put a swagger in my stride!

MADNESS: A FORM OF LOVE
MAX J. LEWY

On many tempestuous nights have I reveled like an awe-struck child,
Frolicking freely through the neon wilderness, or riled.
Greed makes the garbage cans brim bountifully for me,
Yet I exist without the trappings of mainstream materiality.

The moment is forever balanced perfectly within,
And I am the very center of the storm --
The mesmerizing mass-market parade --
The hub of it all. All verse through their nerves,
No stall -- at every stall.
Inwardly still, inwardly me.

About the author:

You think I'm the exception?
One of my comrades in alms is Jesus -- only with breasts --
And another has tunes and tales that could put Tom Waits to the test.

One look at us, sitting with blankets on the sidewalk, and the coldest hearts melt.
We may not be at home in our beds, but are we not more at home in Die Welt?
In this free access condominium beneath the stars,
Love I take in, multiply, and radiate outwards
To the top of skyscrapers down to the shadowy unconscious sea;
Which we homeless embody as the archetype of this poor suffering humanity.
For -- and remember this, ye who build your castles so proud and so tall --
We are all as beggars before the mighty One and All.

Max J. Lewy is the author of "Madness: a form love". A mad-eyed lunatic residing in the mytho-poetic South Wales valleys, letting loose exquisitely choreographed 'howls' against the Mental Hellth System that has so reduced and depraved him. Follow on Twitter :
@ PillPuppetPoet

Shunned by the trance-laden masses,
Spat on by the self-appointed 'elite',
Just around some dirty corner street
In every major city, even today,
In his sleeping bag curled up within
Some dusty back alley passage way...
A Buddha patiently dwells -
Waiting for the world's holy wonder to re-awaken.

***

By lying low on crowded streets,
I rise like warm vapours from vents in the pavement,

Above the multitudinous mind.
I have, I am - everything and nothing:
My words shout surrender, but my voice is filled with design;
Without a penny to my name, the entire city is my boudoir.
For them it is a battleground of all against all.
But pity and gratitude are the portion on which I survive;
Hand-outs to my cupped palms put a swagger in my stride!

On many tempestuous nights have I revelled like an awe-struck child,
Frolicking freely through the neon wilderness, or riled.
Greed makes the garbage cans brim bountifully for me,
Yet I exist without the trappings of mainstream materiality.

The moment is forever balanced perfectly within,
And I am at the very centre of the storm-
The mesmerizing mass-market parade -
The hub of it all. All verve through their nerves,
No stall - at every stall.
Inwardly still, inwardly me.
You think I'm the exception?

One of my comrades in alms is Jesus - only with breasts -
And another has tales and tunes that would put Tom Waits to the test.

One look at us, sitting with blankets on the sidewalk, and the coldest
hearts melt.
We may not be at home in our beds, but are we not more at home in Die
Welt ?
In this free-access condominium beneath the stars,
Love, I take in, multiply and radiate outwards
To the tops of skyscrapers down to the shadowy unconscious sea;
Which we homeless embody as the archetype of this poor suffering
humanity:
For - and remember this, ye who build your castles so proud and so tall -
We are all as beggars before the mighty One And All.

Love's Little Vandal

Love's little vandal
- a pretty criminal, indeed-
Has engraved far the from the driver's station..
In her grotty hinterland
At the back of the bus...
Upon the seats that rust,
Where reluctant riders rest
Their rotund rears...
The holy, miraculous letters
Christened by tears...
Of her true Love's name.

Just another petty crime,
Putting the world to shame.

The Death Of A Flower Girl

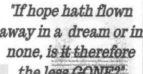

Death Of A Flower Girl

"If hope hath flown away in a dream or in none, is it therefore the less GONE?"

MADNESS: A FORM OF LOVE
Max J. Lewy

I met you in a Church garden, my crude-crafted polygonal character,
crashing into your lovely high-definition pre-rendered flower-bed.
You tended me like one of your dafoldils
Healing me with one of your white magic spells.
I knew from that first moment
That our love would be all too brief.
But little did I know that you would be stolen away
Long before the slick end sequence...
Sweet heroine, with footsteps so soft you hopped into my heart,
I wasn't ready for any love but yours.

Poetry Not Pills

Why, oh why, Sephiroth -- you, who I otherwise loved also as a character --
did you have to cut her down? From that day forth, everything in my life
turned black...
How I searched the internet, hoping to undo

About the
The fateful work of that terrible blade,
Hopelessly cheated and betrayed by fake promises of resurrection... **author:**
Aeris -- your name still hangs on my lips, ringing with tears and regrets my
childish recollection.

Max J. Lewy is the author of 'Madness: a form love'. A mad-eyed lunatic residing in the mytho-poetic South Wales valleys, letting loose exquisitely choreographed 'howls' against the Mental Hellth System that has so reduced and depraved him. Follow on Twitter :
@ PillPuppetPoet

"If hope hath flown away in a dream or in none, is it therefore the less gone?" – Edgar Allen Poe

I met you in a Church garden,
my crude-crafted polygonal character crashing into
your lovely high-definition pre-rendered flower-bed.
You tended me like one of your daffodils
Healing me with one of your white magic spells.
I knew from that first moment
That our love would be all too brief.
But little did I know that you would be stolen away
Long before the slick end sequence...
Sweet heroine, with footsteps so soft you hopped into my heart,

I wasn't ready for any love but yours.
Why, oh why, Sephiroth - you, who I otherwise loved also as a character -
did you have to cut her down? From that day forth, everything in my life
turned black...
How I searched the internet, hoping to undo
The fateful work of that terrible blade,
Hopelessly cheated and betrayed by fake promises of resurrection...
Aeris- your name still hangs on my lips,
ringing with tears and regrets my childish recollection.

Mind Like A Garden

My mind is like a garden. If you go down deep enough there's nothing but dirt and the grave... a solid abyss of immovable rock. But, that doesn't mean it isn't worth growing some pretty flowers here above the earth while I'm there too. Just like breeds of flowers, they are ancient and ineffectual as the hills and still they have their season in which to scatter it with the color, smoothness and vibrancy of petals, each one trembling with early morning dew and the risen beams of the new dawn.

Backstreet Buddha (Lets Fall A Jewel)

I swipe the pockets of the rich;
Relieving them a little of their material burdens.
Without a care, I snitch,
On all society's would-be guardians.
Sitting here, in this ditch,
Having remarkable conversations...
I am pariah, a wicked witch;
Setting his own conflagrations.

Beauty, blessedness, repartee;
Flows in my blood, animates my bones.
As footfalls clatter urgently on these cobblestones...
The sidewalk is my very own settee.

Your funny lives, my T.V.!

Roam the land, sniff the air;
Falling golden silent, I kneel and stare...

Thinking quietly to myself...

"This old world, it will soon be forgotten.
My gown may be dirty,
My skin may be swarthy...
But, also? my Ego ist Toten!

Everything changes, you see,
Everything changes like the river to the sea.
Everything changes, from the shores of Italy,
To the borders of Greece and Turkey.

Ah, yes, Deutschland falls,
And with it Europe, too.
Your consumer kingdom is dead;
Who am I to wail?

An old god says 'Boo!'."

The Wheels Of Samsara

The Wheels Of Samsara

I was once given a bicycle.
It meant the world to me.
To possess its symetrical steely perfection;
Skidding down the city streets at full pelt,
Come rain or sunshine.

I dreamt that one day I would ride far, far away,
Over the horizon, to a whole new world that lay in wait.
It seemed as if my entire life was building up
To just that day, and everything until then
Would just be grey clouds in a bitter sky.

But, that day never came.
The bicycle was smashed into pieces
By on-coming traffic.
From then on, I had to make do with a wheelchair.
Now I spend my days chasing snails
Down the garden path.

MADNESS: A
FORM OF LOVE
MAX J. LEWY

Poetry Not Pills

About the author:

Max J. Lewy is the author of 'Madness: a form
love'. A mad-eyed lunatic residing in the
mytho-poetic South Wales valleys, letting
loose exquisitely choreographed 'howls' against
the Mental Hellth System that has so reduced
and depraved him. Follow on Twitter :
@ PillPuppetPoet

I was once given a bicycle.
It meant the world to me.
To possess its symmetrical steely perfection;
Skidding down the city streets at full pelt,
Come rain or sunshine.

I dreamt that one day I would ride far, far away,
Over the horizon, to a whole new world that lay in wait.
It seemed as if my entire life was building up
To just that day, and everything until then
Would just be grey clouds in a bitter sky.

But, that day never came.
The bicycle was smashed into pieces
By on-coming traffic.
From then on, I had to make do with a wheelchair.
Now I spend my days chasing snails
Down the garden path.

Cherub Rock

The susurrating sea, it glistens;
In this place an angel listens,
Caressing your hair's every lock,
Down by the beautiful Cherub Rock.

Dreams take wing and fancy soars;
The tides echo around the shores,
For eons they have glittered and shook,
Down by the blessed Cherub Rock.

In this place the world forsook,
A secret lies in every nook,
Through the valley, by the brook,

Down by the crag of Cherub Rock.

Once upon some golden morrow,
Came from the sky the god Apollo,
And for a bride, a local beauty took,
Down by the nape of Cherub Rock.

Oh she was a maid so wan and fair,
A glittering jewel so very rare,
A fortunate fate for any man to defrock,
Down by the verdant Cherub Rock.

Soon, after nights sweet and wild,
She became ripe, full with child.
Mighty Apollo, he with triumph shook,
Down by the fateful Cherub Rock.

For a moment she seemed finally happy-
At one with life, this blessed lady.
Giving the crowds a glowing smile,
She danced throughout all Cherub Isle.

Love so strong brings strange things...
The infants arrived- Siamese Twins.

And on their back, they had little wings...

It gave their parents quite a shock,
Down by the innocent Cherub Rock.

A physician arrived, he knew best;
How from one the other the babes to wrest-
How their pinions to nip and tuck,
Down by the watchful Cherub Rock.

But, by Heaven, the plan went wrong,
Young mother, in tears to a funeral song.
Bathed in infant blood, the trees all shook,
Down by the pitiless Cherub Rock.

For years the young bride pined away,
Apollo, from sorrow, he couldn't stay.
It seems a love so wild and free,
Could but end in calamity.

Finally she threw herself
Clinging to their coffin, off the cliff-
Caressing their hair's every lock,
As she fell from the beautiful Cherub Rock...

The susurrating sea, it glistens;
In this place a dead angel listens,
Caressing your hair's every lock,
Down by the cursed Cherub Rock.

Pill Puppet Poet

they plug you full of pills
then give them all the credit
blinding the world to the reality
of one's own inner merit.
they think I'm just
a pill puppet poet!

@pillpuppetpoet on Twitter

Through A Window Paine

The garden flickers from the falling rain,
As I watch silently through a window paine.
Everything in it by Mother carefully arranged,
By tears of the sky today is changed.

A sparrow sits upon a leaftop,
As the cat stalks closer it hops,
And flies away. Just like my luck did
When my wild heart I unhid.

Like rose-bushes, we ourselves must be pruned,
Before we are allowed to blossom and come to bloom.
Sometimes the cutting goes rather too far,
Then it ends in bloody pricks, in stunted men and civil war.

All worship a spirit that is free,
The prophets fall down joyfully,
Upon bended knee!
Heaven is Might, the Sun is Pure;
A savage phase in your offspring,

Indulgently ignore.

You

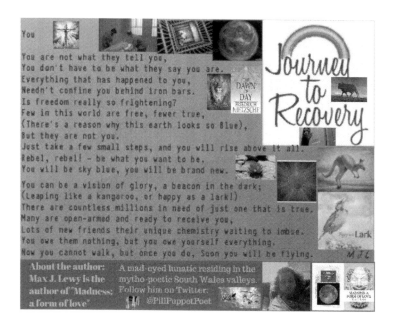

You are not what they tell you,
You don't have to be what they say you are.
Everything that has happened to you,
Needn't confine you behind iron bars.
Is freedom really so frightening?
Few in this world are free, fewer true,
(There's a reason why this earth looks so Blue),
But they are not you.
Just take a few small steps, and you will rise above it all.
Rebel, rebel! - be what you want to be.
You will be sky blue, you will be brand new.
You can be a vision of glory, a beacon in the dark;
(Leaping like a kangaroo, or happy as a lark!)
There are countless millions in need of just one that is true.
Many are open-armed and ready to receive you,
Lots of new friends their unique chemistry waiting to imbue.
You owe them nothing, but you owe yourself everything.
Now you cannot walk, but once you do,
Soon you will be flying.

Sturdy Stalward Stance

Sturdy Stalwart Stance

I stand still and silent.
All around me, the world
Is still too violent.
There is so much to lament.

When God Is Silent

Who will not accuse me if they see me reflect,
Upon the life they have made for me, so misery pecked.

What evil do I conceal?
How far might I go against the Dao?
Isn't to truly *think* to risk it all?

Pecking Order

If they see me turning my back on them,
If they see me turning my gaze to its inner rim
Won't they chase me with raise pitchforks?
Won't they burn me like Guy Fawkes?

To become something I'm not already,
Based upon a moment of chance;

To finally become something I *am*,
Based on a sturdy stalwart stance.

So many worries, I had overcome;
Then the doctors cocked their gun...
Setting my mind back fully asleep,
For another, agonizing decade deep...

Stop in your tracks, and you are deemed crazy, By all around you, unconscious and lazy.

MADNESS: A FORM OF LOVE
Max J. Lewy

Poetry Not Pills

TAO TE CHING

About the author:

Max J. Lewy is the author of "Madness: a form love". A mad-eyed lunatic residing in the mytho-poetic South Wales valleys, letting loose exquisitely choreographed 'howls' against the Mental Hellth System that has so reduced and depraved him. Follow on Twitter :
@ PillPuppetPoet

I stand still and silent.
All around me, the world is still too violent.
There is so much to lament.

Who will not accuse me if they see me reflect,
Upon the life they have made for me, so misery pecked.

What evil do I conceal?
How far might I go against the Tao?
Isn't to truly think to risk it all?

If they see me turning my back on them,
If they see me turning my gaze to its inner rim

Won't they chase me with raised pitchforks?
Won't they burn me like Guy Fawkes?

To become something I'm not already,
Based upon a moment of chance;

To finally become something I *am*
Based on a sturdy stalward stance.

***

So many worries, I had overcome;
Then the doctors cocked their gun...
Setting my mind back fully asleep,
For another, agonzing decade deep...

***

Stop in your tracks, and you are deemed crazy;
By all around you, unconscious and lazy.

Blueberry Bodhisattva

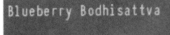

Blueberry Bodhisattva

Calling out his inner God,
With heaps of mackerel pate
and big platters of cod.
Fresh, fastidious, fatty acid Omega 3,
Feeds our brains for the visions we see!
Blueberries and soya milk,
Devoured by those of our ilk.
Our Matcha green tea ceremony,
More sacred than Holy Matrimony.

I touch and transcend my own mortality,
For another day,
if not for eternity.

Knowing ourselves down to the bowels, down to the guts,
Brings greater ecstasy than the emptiest of rituals,
Or the kinkiest of sluts! THIS IS TRUE MEDITATION

About the author:

Max J. Lewy is the author of
"Madness: a form of love"

A mad-eyed lunatic residing in the mytho-poetic South
Wales valleys, letting loose exquisitely choreographed
'howls' against the world and Mental Hellth System.
Follow on Twitter: @PillPuppetPoet

Calling out his inner God,
With heaps of mackerel pate and big platters of cod.
Fresh, fastidious, fatty acid Omega 3,
Feeds our brains for the visions we see!
Blueberries and soya milk,
Devoured by those of our ilk.
Our Matcha green tea ceremony,
More sacred than Holy Matrimony.

Behold, the dietician!

Stringent fasts are such fun.
Getting acquainted with our own vulnerable materiality,
Knowing ourselves down to the bowels, down to the guts,
Brings greater ecstasy than the emptiest of rituals,
Or the kinkiest of sluts!

Nutrition is my religion.
When I eat, I feel God move in me.
I touch and transcend my own mortality,
For another day, if not for eternity.

THIS IS TRUE MEDITATION

All Quiet On The Frontal Lobes

All Quiet On The Frontal Lobes

NO RIGHTS

MADNESS: A FORM OF LOVE

MAX J. LEWY

A battle was fought: his Medulla oblongata versus an electrical socket
The electrical appliance distributors made a racket. So did his screams.
But its pure, scientifically certifed -- who am I to besmirch or mock it?
From now on his ol' rambunctious spirit won't be harboring queer memes.
It'll be pliant, malleable, ductile. The vibrant brio, fizz of magneitc emotion,
Will have dissipated with the deafening circuit of cerebral electrocution.
They'll be no more fuss, no mayhem from his once truculent warrior soul;
The trenches are filled with the fallen, but walking graves no longer howl.

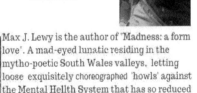

About the author:

Max J. Lewy is the author of "Madness: a form love". A mad-eyed lunatic residing in the mytho-poetic South Wales valleys, letting loose exquisitely choreographed 'howls' against the Mental Hellth System that has so reduced and depraved him. Follow on Twitter :
@ PillPuppetPoet

A battle was fought: his Medulla oblongata versus an electrical socket.
The electrical appliance distributors made a racket. So did his screams.
But its pure, scientifically certified - who am I to besmirch and mock it?
From now on his ol' rumbustious spirit won't be harbouring queer memes.
It'll be pliant, malleable, ductile. The vibrant brio, fizz of magnetic emotion,
Will have dissipated with the deafening circuit of cerebral electrocution.
They'll be no more fuss, no mayhem from his once truculent warrior soul;
The trenches are filled with the fallen, but walking graves no longer howl.

Lost In The Fray

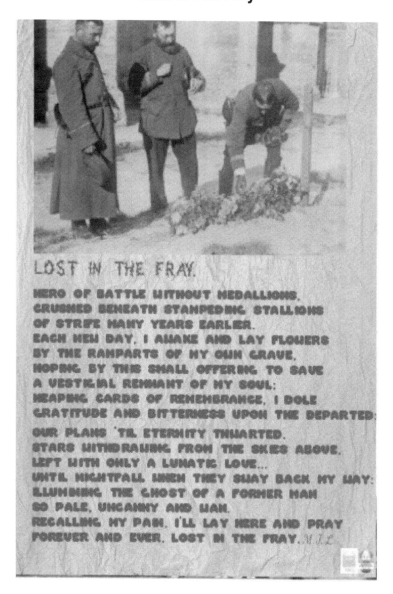

Hero of battle without medallions,
Crushed beneath stampeding stallions
Of strife many years earlier.
Each new day, I awake and lay flowers

By the ramparts of my own grave,
Hoping by this small offering to save
A vestigual remnant of my soul;
Heaping cards of remembrance, I dole
Gratitude and bitterness upon the departed:
Our plans 'til eternity thwarted.
Stars withdrawing from the skies above,
Left with only a lunatic love...
Until nightfall when they sway back my way:
Illumining the ghost of a former man
So pale, uncanny and wan.
Recalling my pain, I'll lay here and pray
Forever and ever, *lost in the fray.*

Rivers of Eternity (For R.W.)

**Rivers Of
Eternity (For
R.W.)**

Two rivers miraculously intertwine ;
Above our heads, the stars align
In all our colorful sins, we are akin:
Two happy lunatics -- one broke free of the bin;
The other, his wild fantasies enabling.

Two rivers miraculously intertwine;
Beneath our eyes, the dew doth shine.
In all our excess glee, you an me
Two happy mad-- one a dearly trapped fairy
The other, longing to set her free.

Love: a madness saner than sanity itself.
Dispensing knowledge like the Oracle at Delphi,
"Who is the wisest in the land?" -- Socrates.
He'll try his best to prove you wrong; never questioning cease.

Two rivers beautifully intertwine;
My soul is yours, your heart is mine.
I'll try my best to prove you wrong,
Let slip the secrets I have held anon
Yet still you hearken to my dark love song.

Two rivers beautifully intertwine;
Words float upon lips, just like wine.
I'll try my best to prove myself false;
Even still, it quickens your pulse.
To my nostrils you are sweet balsam.

Love: a madness more sober than sobriety;
Studying, like Nietzsche, a science of gaiety.
"thou goest to women ? Forgetest not thine whip!"
And I place a lilac on your hip.

Two rivers majestically intertwine;
I can be cruel or I can be kind.
Whichever way, you may swoon.
At my infatuated words --- passion of the moon.
Oh, how I long to cocoon you in my arms.

Two rivers majestically intertwine;
I can be crass ,or I can refined.
You can be shy, or you can brim over:
I still feel luckier than a four leaf clover;
And, besides, my heart tires of being a rover.

Love: a madness more healing than the pill.
"Love is composed of a single soul inhabiting two bodies" -- quoth Aristotle.
Into yours my river, and your s into mine, flows---
Carrying the bitter seeds, fallen from the rushes,

Through Fate's fearful marshes,
Which we both will downstream sow.
To make poppies of our past.

Max James Lewy

Awarded 1st prize
in RealistcPoetry's
""Perspectives Of Love"
Poetry 2018 Contest.

From the collection "Madness: a form of love"

Rivers Of
Eternity (For
R.W.)

Two rivers miraculously intertwine ;
Above our heads, the stars align.
In all our colorful sins, we are akin:
Two happy lunatics -- one broke free of the bin;
The other, his wild fantasies enabling.

Two rivers miraculously intertwine;
Beneath our eyes, the dew doth shine.
In all our excess glee, you an me
Two happy mad-- one a dearly trapped fairy
The other, longing to set her free.

Love: a madness saner than sanity itself.
Dispensing knowledge like the Oracle at Delphi.
"Who is the wisest in the land?" -- Socrates.
He'll try his best to prove you wrong; never questioning cease.

Two rivers beautifully intertwine;
My soul is yours, your heart is mine.
I'll try my best to prove you wrong;
Let slip the secrets I have held anon
Yet still you hearken to my dark love song.

Two rivers beautifully intertwine;
Words float upon lips, just like wine.
I'll try my best to prove myself false;
Even still, it quickens your pulse.
To my nostrils you are sweet balsam.

Love: a madness more sober than sobriety;
Studying, like Nietzsche, a science of gaiety.
"thou goest to women ? Forgetest not thine whip!"
And I place a lilac on your hip.

Two rivers majestically intertwine;
I can be cruel or I can be kind.
Whichever way, you may swoon.
At my infatuated words -- passion of the moon.
Oh, how I long to cocoon you in my arms.

Two rivers majestically intertwine;
I can be crass ,or I can refined.
You can be shy, or you can brim over;
I still feel luckier than a four leaf clover:
And, besides, my heart tires of being a rover

Love: a madness more healing than the pill.
"Love is composed of a single soul inhabiting two bodies" -- quoth Aristotle.
Into yours my river, and your s into mine, flows--
Carrying the bitter seeds, fallen from the rushes,

Through Fate's fearful marshes,
Which we both will downstream sow,
To make poppies of our past.

Max James Lewy

ABOUT THE AUTHOR

Max J. Lewy (1983-) was born in the ex-coal-mining area of the South Wales valleys, U.K. to a Jewish father and English mother, and is now a recovering patient of Mental Health System abuses. He studied Philosophy at Warwick University, undergoing a spiritual transition and potential breakthrough which was aborted and derailed by misplaced 'treatment'. He spent 6 months living on the street as a runaway from NHS 'services' in Brighton. He self-published his first book of poetry, "Madness: a form of love" last year, detailing his ordeals as a form of therapy (#PoetryNotPills #MeditationNotSedation) and defence, and is the winner of RealisticPoetry's 2018 "Perspectives Of Love" Poetry Contest for the poem "River Of Eternity (For R. W.)". While currently spending his time writing poetry and philosophy about Mental Health, he is also considering re-training to work in the field of Artificial Intelligence (although, as he says himself, his intelligence is already highly artificial!). In his spare time, he plays tennis, drinks pure cacao sweetened with Manuka Honey, a long with various other herbal remedies and holistic health rituals, and avoids doctors at all costs.

@GaslitByAMadman
(On Twitter & Gab)

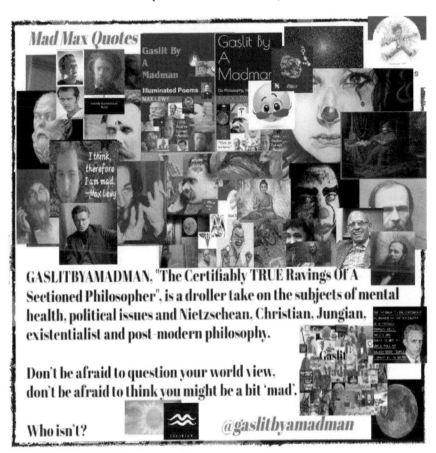

GASLITBYAMADMAN, "The Certifiably TRUE Ravings Of A Sectioned Philosopher", is a droller take on the subjects of mental health, political issues and Nietzschean, Christian, Jungian, existentialist and post-modern philosophy.

Don't be afraid to question your world view, don't be afraid to think you might be a bit 'mad'.

Who isn't?   @gaslitbyamadman

On YouTube

@MadTruths on Minds.com

gaslitbyamadman.home.blog
on WordPress

"Men have called me mad; but the question is not settled whether madness is or is not the loftiest intelligence -- whether much that is glorious -- whether all that is profound -- does not spring from disease of thought -- from moods of mind exalted at the expense of the general intellect. They who dream by day are cognizant of many things which escape those who only dream by night.
— Edgar Allan Poe, "Eleonora"   @gaslitbyamadman